D0096327

Dutch cooking today

 Het Nederlands Zuivelbureau

Contents

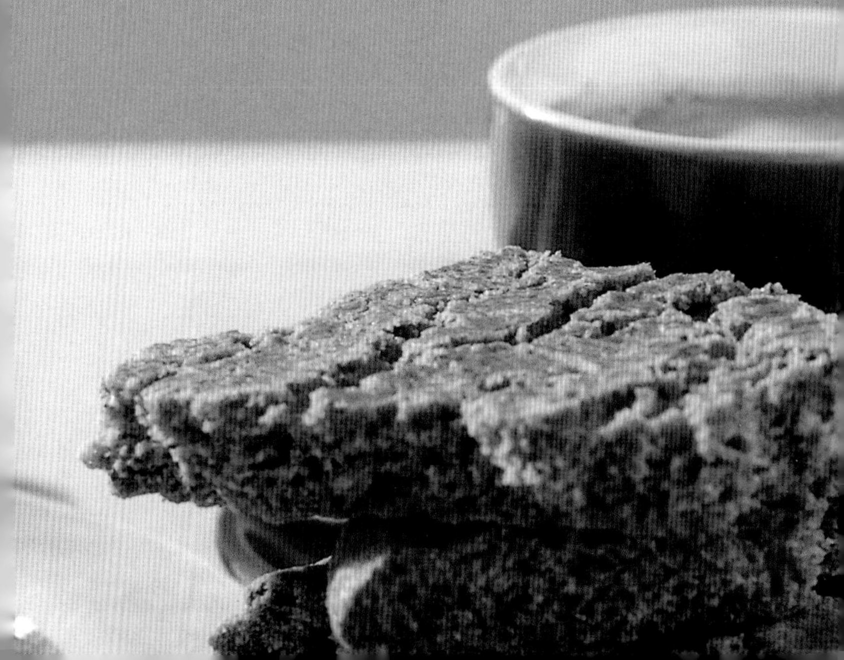

Tasty Dutch cooking with a few well-chosen sauces

You may not realise when leafing through all those cookery articles and magazines that the Dutch still enjoy eating Dutch food. Or perhaps we should say, are eating Dutch food *again*. Red cabbage with apples, stew, brown beans with bacon, one-pan winter warmers, cauliflower in a sauce... This book is brimming with Dutch classic dishes, all prepared in a modern and lighter way than in Grandma's day. There are even different versions of all the favourites. Evergreens like *hete bliksem* (Dutch apple and mash), shepherd's pie and *boerenkoolstamppot* (Dutch curley kale and mash) have been given delicious new twists to suit today's more sophisticated palate. And going back to that cauliflower in a sauce: here follows five classic, quick and easy sauces to lift all those good honest meat, fish or chicken dishes into something really special!

How much sauce

The amount of sauce served depends on the specific dish. For instance, more sauce is need for rice, pasta or boiled potatoes than when sautéed or chipped potatoes are on the menu. It is also a matter of individual taste. Some like to swamp their meal with sauce, while others are happy with one or two tablespoons. A rule of thumb is 100 – 125 ml/$3^1/2$ - 5 fl oz sauce per person.

Cheese sauce (for vegetables)
25 g/1 oz butter
25 g/1 oz plain flour
$1/4$ litre/$1/2$ pint milk
75-100 g/$3^1/2$ oz mature Gouda (or Cheddar) cheese, grated
salt and freshly ground pepper
nutmeg (optional)

• Heat the butter in a saucepan and stir in the flour. Cook gently for 2 or 3 minutes, stirring frequently to prevent the roux turning brown or burning.
• Slowly add the milk a little at a time and remain stirring until the sauce comes to the boil and is thick and smooth. Add the cheese and stir the sauce until melted.
• Season to taste with salt, pepper and optional nutmeg.

Prawn sauce (for fish)
25 g/1 oz butter
25 g/1 oz plain flour
$1/4$ litre/$1/2$ pint fish stock
75 g/3 oz Dutch prawns
2-3 tablespoons double cream
salt and freshly ground pepper

• Heat the butter in a saucepan and stir in the flour. Cook gently for 2 or 3 minutes, stirring frequently to prevent the roux turning brown or burning.

• Slowly add the stock a little at a time and remain stirring until the sauce comes to the boil and is thick and smooth.
• Simmer for a further 1 or 2 minutes and season to taste. Enrich with cream and stir in the prawns until heated through.

Red wine sauce (for red meat)
30 g/1oz butter (or fat from the meat)
2 finely chopped shallots
25 g/1oz plain flour
250 ml/10 fl oz meat stock
100 ml/3^1/$_2$ fl oz red wine
^{1}/$_2$ teaspoon sugar
salt and freshly ground pepper

• Heat the butter in a saucepan and fry the shallots, scraping away any that stick to the bottom of the pan.
• Stir in the flour and continue stirring while pouring in the meat stock. Bring to the boil and cook for a few more minutes.
• Pour in the wine and season to taste with sugar, salt and pepper.

Cream of mushroom sauce (for white meat)
35 g/1oz butter (or fat from the meat)
1 finely chopped small onion
150 g/5 oz mushrooms
100 ml/3^1/$_2$ fl oz water
125 ml/5 fl oz cream
2 teaspoons plain flour
salt and freshly ground pepper
1 tablespoon finely chopped parsley

Heat the butter and fry the onions and mushrooms for about 5 minutes. Mix the flour and the water until a smooth paste. Pour into the pan, scraping away any vegetables from the bottom of the pan. Stir in the cream and bring everything slowly to the boil. Simmer for 5 minutes. Add the parsley and season to taste.

Orange and thyme sauce (for chicken and game)
1 finely chopped shallot
15 g/^{1}/$_2$ oz butter
2 tablespoons fresh thyme or 2 teaspoons dry thyme
100 ml/3^1/$_2$ fl oz thick chicken or game stock
100 ml/3^1/$_2$ fl oz vegetable stock
200 ml/7 oz orange juice
125 ml/5 fl oz crème fraîche
salt and freshly ground pepper

• Heat the butter and fry the onion. Stir in the thyme, stock and orange juice. Bring to the boil and simmer until reduced by one half.
• Stir in the crème fraîche and continue cooking for a few minutes.
• Season to taste with salt and pepper.

Poffertjes: Tiny cheese pancakes with herb butter

400 ml/14 fl oz milk
15 g/^{1}/$_2$ oz fresh yeast or 7 g/^{1}/$_2$ teaspoon dried yeast
200 g/7 oz flour
100 g/3^1/$_2$ oz buckwheat flour
pinch salt
1 egg
100 g/3^1/$_2$ oz mature Gouda or other full-flavoured cheese
freshly ground pepper
40 g/1^1/$_2$ oz melted butter
For the herb butter:
125 g/4 oz softened butter
1 tablespoon lemon juice
1 teaspoon finely chopped parsley
1 teaspoon finely chopped chives
1 teaspoon finely chopped chervil

Preparation/cooking: approx. 25 minutes

About 1 hour for the batter to rise

Contains per serving: 3434 kJ/ 823 kcal. 20 g protein, 50 g fat, 74 g carbo-hydrate

Variation
Make a batter without adding grated cheese, and serve the 'poffertjes' with stoned prunes, a dash of red port and lots of icing sugar.

Preparation. Combine the butter, lemon juice and herbs in a bowl. Leave to stand until further use.
• Warm the milk until tepid. Crumble or sprinkle the yeast into a small bowl, add a splash of milk and mix until smooth. In a bowl mix the flour, buckwheat flour, salt, yeast mixture, egg and the remaining tepid milk with a whisk until a smooth batter. Use the whisk to remove any lumps. Cover and leave to rise for 1 hour in a warm place.
• Stir the grated cheese and pepper into the batter.
Cooking. Lightly grease the 'poffertjes' pan and fill the depressions about half way with the batter. Quickly fry the tiny pancakes and when golden and almost dry turn and repeat until both sides are cooked.
• Serve the pancakes with a small lump of herb butter.
• Delicious with halved cherry tomatoes.

For this recipe you need a traditional 'poffertjes' pan or else increase milk to ^{3}/$_4$ litre and bake small pancakes with 1-2 tablespoons of batter.

Brabant sausage rolls

1/2 packet white bread mix
50 g/2 oz softened butter
150 ml/5 fl oz tepid water
salt
50 g/2 oz mature Gouda (or Cheddar) cheese, grated
For the filling:
1 egg
2 cloves garlic
200 g/7 oz minced beef and pork
2 tablespoons breadcrumbs
salt and freshly ground pepper
2 tablespoons finely chopped mixed herbs (thyme, parsley and oregano)
1 – 2 tablespoons flour

Preparation/cooking: approx. 30/20 minutes

25 minutes for dough to rise

Contains per serving: 955 kJ/ 229 kcal. 9 g protein, 13 g fat, 18 g carbohydrate

Preparation. Combine the bread mix with the butter, water and a pinch of salt in a bowl. Knead thoroughly until smooth and elastic. Cover with a tea towel and leave to rise for 25 minutes in a warm place.

• Meanwhile make the filling. Beat the egg in a small bowl and put 2 tablespoons aside for brushing the rolls later. Peel and finely chop the garlic. In a bowl combine the mince with the beaten egg, garlic, breadcrumbs, salt, pepper and herbs.

• Form mince into 8 sausages about 10 cm (4 in) in length and roll in the flour.

• Heat the oven to 200 °C/400 °F.

• Roll dough into an oblong on a lightly floured work surface and cut into 8: 10 x 15 cm (4 x 6 in) pieces. Wet the edges of the dough, place each sausage on a piece of dough, roll over and firmly seal edges.

Cooking. Brush the sausage rolls with the remaining egg and sprinkle grated cheese on top. Place on a lined baking tray and bake for about 20 minutes until golden brown and cooked.

Variations

* Spice the mince with a finely chopped clove garlic, 1 teaspoon chilli powder and 1 tablespoon tomato puree.
* Sprinkle the sausage rolls with sesame seeds.

4 SERVINGS

DUTCH BREAKFAST, BRUNCH AND LUNCH

Wentelteefjes: French toast with lemon

1 egg
grated rind of lemon*
150 ml/5 fl oz milk
4 slices stale white bread
30 g/1oz butter
2 tablespoons soft, brown sugar

*Preparation/cooking: approx.
15 minutes*

*Contains per serving: 804 kJ/192 kcal.
5 g protein, 9 g fat, 22 g carbohydrate*

* or 2 teaspoons cinnamon.

Variations
• *Substitute the sugar and serve
the French toast with jam, fried
apple or grated coconut.*
• *Substitute current bread for white
bread and serve the toast with
icing sugar and segments of pear
fried in butter.*

Preparation. Beat the egg in a bowl and stir in the grated zest of lemon and milk. Remove crusts from the bread.
• Dip the slices of bread in the egg mixture, placing each slice one on top of the other in the bowl. Make sure the bread absorbs all the liquid.
Cooking. Heat the butter in a large frying pan and fry the bread over a moderate heat on both sides until nicely golden brown.
• Serve the french toast with soft brown sugar.

Three-in-a-pan with orange and cinnamon sugar

200 g/7 oz self-rising flour
salt
1 egg
200 ml/7 fl oz milk
juice and zest of 1 orange, grated
2 teaspoons cinnamon
100 g/3¹/² oz sugar
30 g/1 oz butter

Preparation/cooking: approx. 10/15 minutes

Contains per serving: 1589 kJ/ 376 kcal. 9 g protein, 9 g fat, 65 g carbohydrate

Variation
Add 50 g/2 oz of raisins and 1 finely diced Cox's apple to the batter. Serve the pancakes with honey.

Preparation. Sieve the flour with a pinch of salt into a bowl. Add the egg and half the milk and mix until a smooth batter. While stirring, thin out the batter with the remaining milk. Stir in the orange juice and grated zest.
• Combine the cinnamon and sugar in a small bowl.
Cooking. Heat the butter in a frying pan and add three heaped spoonfuls of batter. Bake the three-in-a-pan over moderate heat until light brown, then turn and bake on the other side until golden brown. Repeat the process with the remaining batter. Keep the pancakes warm.
• Serve with cinnamon sugar.
• Delicious with a liberal spoonful of marmalade.

Tomatoes stuffed with egg salad

4 anchovy fillets
3 tablespoons milk
4 medium tomatoes
4 hard-boiled eggs
100 ml/3^1/$_2$ oz crème fraîche
50 ml/2 fl oz mayonnaise
freshly ground pepper
2 tablespoons finely chopped
chives + extra for garnishing or
1 tablespoon drained capers or
black imitation caviar

*Preparation/serving: approx.
15/5 minutes
Contains per serving: 1117 kJ/270 kcal.
10 g protein, 25 g fat, 2 g carbohydrate*

Preparation. Soak the anchovy fillets for 10 minutes in milk. Slice the tops off the tomatoes and gently hollow out with a spoon or grapefruit knife. Drain upside down on paper towel. Remove the anchovy fillets from the milk and also drain on paper towel.
• Chop the eggs and anchovy fillets into small pieces and mix with the crème fraîche, mayonnaise, chives and pepper.
To serve. Stuff the tomatoes with the egg salad and garnish with chives and capers.
• Delicious with hot toast.

Variation
Add 50 g/2 oz chopped stoned black olives and four chopped sundried tomatoes in oil to the egg salad. Substitute fresh chopped basil leaves for the chives.

Russian salad

150 g/5 oz piece of cooked beef
or shoulder ham
150 g/5 oz cooked potatoes
125 g/4 oz cooked beetroot
1/2 red pepper
1/2 sweet apple
1 tablespoon white wine
vinegar
1 small tub crème fraîche
4 small gherkins
2 hardboiled eggs
1 tablespoon finely chopped
parsley
1 tablespoon finely chopped dill
salt and freshly ground pepper
1 lettuce

*Preparation/serving: approx.
20 minutes*
*Contains per serving: 1198 kJ/288 kcal.
18 g protein, 19 g fat, 11 g carbohydrate*

Preparation. Cut the meat, potatoes, beetroot, pepper and apple into small cubes. Mix everything together in a large bowl with the wine vinegar and crème fraîche.

• Thinly slice the gherkins and eggs and add to the salad along with the herbs.

• Add seasoning to taste.

To serve: arrange the salad on a bed of lettuce.

Variations
* Garnish the salad with small cocktail onions, gherkins and egg.
* Substitute the meat for 150 g/ 5 oz prawns. Season the salad with cayenne instead of ground pepper and serve on 75 g/3 oz rucola.

DUTCH BREAKFAST, BRUNCH AND LUNCH

4 SERVINGS

Uitsmijter: Fried ham and eggs with mustard cheese

25 g/1 oz butter + butter for spreading
4 eggs
4 slices Dutch mustard cheese (or mustard Cheddar)
salt and freshly ground pepper
4 slices wholemeal farmhouse bread
100 g/3½ oz raw ham, sliced
4 gherkins split into 'fans'
2 tomatoes cut into four
finely chopped parsley

Preparation/cooking: approx. 10 minutes

Contains per serving: 1618 kJ/388 kcal. 22 g protein, 26 g fat, 16 g carbohydrate

Preparation. Melt the butter in a large frying pan, break the eggs into the pan and cook for a few minutes over a low heat.
• Divide a slice of mustard cheese around each yolk and add seasoning to taste. Cover the pan and cook the eggs for a few minutes until done and the cheese has melted.
To serve. Toast the slices of bread and spread with butter. Divide the ham across the bread and top off with a fried egg. Garnish with gherkin, tomato and parsley.

Variation

Instead of ham, fry slices of chorizo with the eggs and cover the bread with slices of non-crumbly goats cheese. Garnish with a red pepper and sweetpepper-corn salad and green olives.

4 SERVINGS

2 waxy potatoes
100 g/3½ oz mushrooms
100 g/3½ oz piece smoked
bacon, diced
100 /3½ oz frozen peas
1 tablespoon finely chopped
parsley
1 tablespoon finely chopped
chives
6 eggs
100 ml/3½ fl oz milk
salt and freshly ground pepper

*Preparation/cooking: approx.
25 minutes*

*Contains per serving: 1145 kJ/275 kcal.
18 g protein, 18 g fat, 11 g carbohydrate*

Variations
* Quickly sauté thick slices of
tomato in hot butter. Garnish each
omelette wedge with tomato and a
sprinkling of grated cheese.
Pop under a grill
until melted.

Preparation. Dice the potatoes and slice the mushrooms. Cook the potatoes in hot water with a pinch of salt for about 10 minutes until tender. Fry the diced bacon in a large frying pan. Remove and fry the diced potato in the bacon fat for about 5 minutes.

• Add the mushrooms, peas, bacon and herbs to the potato and continue cooking.

• Beat the eggs and milk in a bowl and add seasoning to taste.

• Pour the mixture into the pan along with the vegetables. Cook over a low heat until the omelette thickens. Lift the edges of the omelette with a fork from time to time so that the uncooked mixture runs underneath and sets.

To serve. Cut the omelette in 4 wedges and serve on individual plates.

• Delicious with chunks of fresh farmhouse bread and tomato sauce.

Variation
Substitute cooked mussels for the bacon, but only add these to the
omelette when it is almost cooked.

Boterkoek: Butter cake with apricot filling

250 g/8 oz flour
175 g/6 oz white castor sugar
salt
225 g/7 oz chilled butter
100 g/3½ oz soaked dried apricots
50 g/2 oz flaked almonds
2 tablespoons ginger syrup
1 tablespoon milk

Preparation/cooking: approx.
15/20 minutes

Contains per serving: 1558 kJ/373 kcal.
4 g protein, 21 g fat, 42 g carbohydrate

Variation
Finely slice 10 balls of stem ginger and mix into the dough. Bake the butter biscuit without the filling.

Preparation. Preheat the oven to 200 °C/400 °F.
• In a bowl combine flour, sugar and a pinch of salt. Cut the butter into pieces and mix into the flour. Then using two knives cut them into smaller pieces through the flour. Knead the fat and flour together with one cool hand and gather up into a firm dough ball. This is also easily done in a food processor.
• Cut the apricots in small pieces and mix them in a bowl with the almonds and ginger syrup.
• Press half the dough into a 24 cm/10 in round pie dish. Spread the apricot mixture over the top. Roll out the other half on a lightly floured work surface until it is the same size as the dish. Place over the apricot filling, firmly pressing the pastry edges together.
• Using the blunt side of a knife, decorate the dough with cross-hatch markings and brush with milk.
• Bake the butter cake in the oven for 15-20 minutes until cooked and golden brown.
To serve. Allow to cool and just before serving slice the cake into wedges.

Dutch apple pie

300 g/10 oz flour
125 g/4 oz white castor sugar
salt
200 g/7 oz chilled butter
1 egg yolk
100 g/3½ oz raisins
100 ml/3½ fl oz orange juice
1 kg/2 lb firm apples (Elstar, Jonagold)
2 teaspoons custard powder
2 teaspoons cinnamon
2 tablespoons sugar
3 tablespoons apricot jam

Preparation/cooking: approx. 45/45 minutes

Contains per serving: 1708 kJ/407 kcal. 4 g protein, 18 g fat, 58 g carbohydrate

Variations

Bake the cake in a less deep cake tin (26-28cm/10-12 in). Cut 6 Amaretti biscuits into small pieces and mix into the apple mixture.

Instead of the pastry strips sprinkle 50 g/2 oz flaked almonds and 2 tablespoons of sugar over the cake.

• *Delicious with whipped cream or vanilla custard.*

Preparation. In a bowl combine flour, sugar and a pinch of salt. Cut the butter into pieces and mix into the flour. Then using two knives cut the butter into smaller pieces through the flour. Knead the fat and flour together with one cool hand and roll up into a firm dough ball. This is also easily done in a food processor.

• Grease a 24 cm/10 in cake tin with a false bottom, and press ⅔ of the dough into the bottom and sides of the tin. Refrigerate the tin and remaining dough until ready to use.

• Preheat the oven to 175 ⁰C/375 ⁰F. In a saucepan bring the raisins and orange juice to the boil and leave to simmer gently for about 5 minutes until the liquid has evaporated.

• Peel, core and slice the apples. Put them in a bowl and combine with the raisins, custard powder, cinnamon and sugar. Arrange the filling over the cake base.

• Roll out the rest of the dough on a floured work surface and cut into 1 cm/½ in strips. Arrange in a criss-cross pattern on top of the apple mixture, pressing them down at the edges of the tin.

• Place the apple cake in the lower part of the oven and bake for about 45 minutes until golden brown and cooked. Remove cake from the oven and brush with apricot jam so that the pastry shines. Allow to cool in the cake tin for 10 minutes.

To serve. Remove from the tin and serve on a flat dish.

Limburg cherry crumble flan

175 g/6^1/$_2$ oz butter
375 g/13 oz flour
200 g/7 oz sugar
1 packet of dried yeast
salt
3 egg yolks
3 ml/10 fl oz milk
1 vanilla pod
2 tablespoons custard powder or
cornflour
2 pots of stoned cherries
3 tablespoons wild fruit or
blackberry jam
icing sugar

Preparation/cooking: approx. 1 hour
To rise: 1 hour

Contains per serving: 1671 kJ/398 kcal.
6 g protein, 17 g fat, 55 g carbohydrate

Variations
* Substitute a tin of apricots for
the cherries
* Make a nut topping by adding 50
g/2 oz of finely chopped hazelnuts
to the crumble mix.

Preparation. Melt 50 g/2 oz butter. Using a food processor or hand mixer with dough hooks, combine 250 g/8 oz flour, 25 g/1 oz sugar, yeast , pinch of salt, 1 egg yolk, 50 ml/2 fl oz tepid milk and the melted butter to a smooth and elastic dough. Knead this with the hand for a further 5 minutes. Place in a bowl covered with clingfilm and leave in a warm place for about 45 minutes to rise.

• Split the vanilla pod lengthwise. Heat the remaining milk with the vanilla pod in a saucepan and simmer for about 10 minutes to extract the vanilla flavour. In a bowl beat the remaining egg yolks with 100 g/3^1/$_2$ oz sugar until mixture is creamy. Beat in the custard powder and 3 tablespoons of the hot vanilla milk.

• Remove the vanilla pod from the milk, scrape out the black seeds and stir into the milk. While stirring, add the yolk mixture and continue stirring until the custard thickens. Away from the heat, beat 50 g/2 oz butter into the custard sauce. Allow to cool.

• Heat the oven to 200 ºC/ 400 ºF. Drain the cherries in a sieve. In a bowl combine these with the jam. Grease a 28-30 cm/12 in flan tin. Roll out the dough on a floured work surface until about ^{1}/$_2$ cm/ ^{1}/$_4$ in thick. Line the dish with the dough, pressing it firmly against the rim.

• Spread the custard sauce over the base and arrange the cherries on top. Place 125 g/4 oz flour, 75 g/3oz sugar and 75 g/3 oz butter cut into pieces in a bowl and rub together with the tips of your fingers until a crumbly dough. Sprinkle the crumble topping over the custard filling.

• Place the custard flan in the lower part of the oven and bake for about 25-30 minutes until golden brown and cooked. Allow to cool in the tin.

To serve. Just before serving dust the flan with icing sugar.

Speculaas: Spiced biscuit

MAKES 500 G/1 LB

200 g/7 oz self-raising cake flour
125 g/4 oz brown soft sugar
2 tablespoons all spice
pinch salt
150 g/5 oz chilled butter
1 tablespoon milk

Preparation/cooking: approx.
45 minutes
To rest: 1 day
Contains per serving: 1908 kJ/456 kcal.
4 g protein, 25 g fat, 53 g carbohydrate

Variations

*Wholemeal spiced biscuit. Substi-
tute wholemeal flour for self-rai-
sing flour plus 1/2 packet of baking
powder.

*Almond spiced biscuit. Line a cake
tin with half the dough, spread the
base with 300 g/10 oz almond paste
thinned with 3 tablespoons lemon
juice and cover with the rest of the
dough. Sprinkle flaked almonds on
top and bake for 30-40 minutes.

Preparation. In a bowl combine the cake flour, brown sugar, all spice and a pinch of salt. Cut the butter into pieces and mix into the flour. Then using two knives cut them into smaller pieces through the flour. Add the milk and quickly knead the fat and flour together with one cool hand to form a firm dough ball. This is also easily done in a food processor.

• Wrap the dough in clingfilm and allow to rest in a cool place for at least 2 hours, but preferably for a day to draw out the spice flavour.

• Preheat the oven to 175 °C/375 °F. Roll out the dough into a rectangle about 1 cm/1/2 in thick. Place this (or two smaller rectangles) onto a lined baking tray and bake the spiced biscuit in the oven for about 30 minutes until done.

• Cool the biscuit on a wire rack.

To serve. Break the biscuit into pieces and place on a flat serving dish.

Smoked eel appetizers

1 lemon
50 g/2 oz softened butter
2 tablespoons finely chopped
chives
salt and freshly ground pepper
3 slices white tin-loaf
100 g/3^1/$_2$ oz smoked eel at
room temperature

*Preparation/serving: approx.
10 minutes*

*Contains per serving: 280 kJ/67 kcal.
2 g protein, 5 g fat, 3 g carbohydrate*

Preparation. Cut 3 thick slices of lemon and cut again into quarters. Grate 1 teaspoon lemon rind into a small bowl. Add the butter, chives, few drops lemon, salt and pepper to taste and mix well.
• Toast the slices of bread and cut into quarters. Cut the smoked eel into 12 equal pieces.
To serve. Spread the chive butter onto the toast squares and place a piece of smoked eel on each. Garnish with pieces of lemon and serve on a dish.

Herring appetizers in mustard cream

2 raw young herrings
2 spring onions
125 ml/5 fl oz crème fraîche
1 teaspoon smooth mustard
salt and freshly ground pepper
^{1}/$_2$ red onion
12 Melba toasts or small rounds
of rye bread

*Preparation/serving: approx.
10 minutes*

*Contains per serving: 323 kJ/78 kcal.
5 g protein, 6 g fat, 1 g carbohydrate*

Preparation. Remove the tails from the herrings and most of the small bones. Cut the herring into thin pieces. Slice the spring onions into thin rings.
• In a bowl combine the crème fraîche, mustard and half the spring onions.
• Mix in the pieces of herring, adding salt and pepper to taste. Peel and finely chop half the red onion.
To serve. Spread the herring in mustard cream onto the toast or rounds of rye bread and garnish with red onion and remaining spring onions. Serve the herring appetizers on a dish.

Cheese puffs

40 g/1$\frac{1}{2}$ oz butter
$\frac{1}{2}$ teaspoon curry powder
25 g/1 oz flour
2 ml/7 fl oz milk
100 g/3$\frac{1}{2}$ oz mature Gouda or
Cheddar cheese, grated
8 sheets of frozen cream puff
pastry
1 tomato
2 spring onions
25 g/1 oz mature Gouda cheese
or any full-flavoured cheese,
grated and/or 2 tablespoons
sesame seeds

*Preparation/cooking: approx.
25/20 minutes*

*Contains per serving: 3295kJ/793 kcal.
18 g protein, 61 g fat, 44 g carbohydrate*

Variation
*Use the same method to make
small cheese turnovers. Cut the puff
pastry sheets into four, spoon a
tablespoon of cheese sauce onto
each and fold double. Then follow
the recipe as before.*

Preparation. Preheat the oven to 200 ºC/400 ºF.
Place the individual sheets of puff pastry on the
work surface to thaw.
• Melt 25 g/1 oz butter in a saucepan and briefly
fry the curry powder. Mix in the flour and gradually
add the milk while stirring. Continue stirring until
the sauce thickens and cook gently for another
5 minutes. Remove pan from the heat and add the
grated cheese. Leave to cool. Plunge the tomato in
boiling water for 30 seconds. Lift off the skin, de-
seed and roughly chop the tomato. Drain the
pieces of tomato on paper towel. Slice the spring
onions into rings, wash and then drain in a sieve.
• Fold the tomato and spring onions into the cheese
sauce. Divide each pastry sheet in two and make an
incision every centimetre (or half inch) along one
half of the sheets. Spread the cheese mixture over
the other half of the sheets to within 1 cm/$\frac{1}{2}$ in
of the pastry edge. Melt the remaining butter and
brush pastry edges. Place the incised pastry sheets
on top and firmly press edges together.
• Place the cheese puffs on a lined baking tray
and brush with melted butter. Sprinkle with cheese
powder and/or sesame seeds.
• Bake in the middle of the oven for 20 minutes
until golden brown and cooked.
To serve. Delicious with a tomato dip sauce.

Bitterballen: Bite-size croquettes

200 g/7 oz stewing beef or
shoulder of veal, cubed
1 bouquet garni
400 ml/14 fl oz beef stock
(from 1 stock cubes)
30 g/1 oz butter
30 g/1 oz flour
salt and freshly ground pepper
nutmeg
2 eggs
100 g/3^1/2 oz breadcrumbs
groundnut or sunflower oil for
frying
coarse mustard

Preparation/cooking: approx. 1^1/2 hours
Contains per serving: 168 kJ/40 kcal.
3 g protein, 2 g fat, 4 g carbohydrate

Variations
Bite-size cheese croquettes. Make a
white sauce with 30/1 oz, 30 g/
1 oz flour and 200 ml/7 fl oz milk.
Stir in 200 g/7 oz of mature Gouda
or Cheddar cheese and 3 table-
spoons chopped chives.

Preparation. In a pan bring the meat, bouquet garni and beef stock slowly to the boil and simmer for about 1 hour until meat is tender.
• Strain off 200 ml/7 fl oz stock into a measuring jug. Slice the cooked meat very thinly.
• Melt the butter in a pan and stir in the flour. Add the stock, while stirring, and continue stirring until the sauce is thick and smooth. Leave the sauce to cook gently for about 2 minutes. Stir in the meat and add salt, pepper and nutmeg to taste.
• Pour the ragout onto a flat plate and refrigerate until firm.
• In a deep plate beat the eggs with one tablespoon of water. Shape the ragout into 24 balls and roll in the breadcrumbs. Then roll in the beaten egg and bread-crumbs again. Repeat until well coated.
• Heat oil in a deep fat fryer to 180 °C/350 °F. Deep fry the croquettes 6 at a time for 3-4 minutes until brown and crisp. Drain on paper towel.
To serve. Place the bite-size croquettes on a serving dish and serve with coarse mustard.

Bite-size shrimp croquettes. Make a white sauce with 30 g/1 oz butter, 30 g/1 oz flour, 200 ml/7 fl oz fish stock and 2 tablespoons lemon juice. Stir in 200 g/7 oz chopped shrimps, 2 tablespoons finely chopped parsley and 1 tablespoon freshly chopped dill.

Zebras

**100 g/3¹/₂ oz softened butter
200 g/7 oz cream cheese
100 g/3¹/₂ oz mature cheese, grated
salt and freshly ground pepper
8 slices rye bread**

*Preparation/serving: approx.
10 minutes
To firm up: 1 hour
Contains per serving: 602 kJ/145 kcal.
4 g protein, 11 g fat, 8 g carbohydrate*

Preparation. With a mixer beat the butter and cream cheese together until fluffy. Sprinkle in the grated cheese and add salt and pepper to taste.
• Thickly spread the cheese mixture over 6 slices of rye bread. Place two spreaded slices on top of another two and repeat, so that you have two triple-layers. Cover with the two non-spreaded slices and press down. Wrap the layers in clingfilm and refrigerate for about 1 hour until firm.
To serve. Slice each layer with a sharp knife into 8 pieces and place on a serving dish.

Variations

*Salmon zebras. Substitute 100 g/3¹/₂ oz snippets of smoked salmon for the cheese and add 1 tablespoon finely chopped dill to the cream cheese filling. Use a different kind of non-white bread like pumpernickel.
*Tuna zebras. Substitute ¹/₂ can drained tuna fish, 1 tablespoon finely chopped basil and 1 teaspoon finely chopped capers for 50 g/2 oz grated cheese.

Cauliflower soup with cheese puffs

1 large potato
1 onion
25 g/1 oz butter
500 g/1 lb cauliflower florets +
one or two for garnishing
1 litre/2 pints vegetable stock
100 ml/3^1/$_2$ fl oz cream
pinch nutmeg
salt and freshly ground pepper
2 tablespoons finely chopped
parsley
For the cheese puffs:
50 ml/2 fl oz milk
25 g/1 oz butter
30 g/1 oz flour
1 egg, beaten
2 tablespoons mature Gouda
cheese or any full-flavoured
cheese, grated

Preparation/serving: approx.
45 minutes/5 minutes
Contains per serving: 1182 kJ/284 kcal.
8 g protein, 22 g fat, 14 g carbohydrate

Preparation. Peel and cut the potato into cubes. Peel and finely chop the onion. Heat the butter in a large pan and fry the onion and potato for about 3 minutes. Add the cauliflower florets and vegetable stock and simmer for 10-15 minutes.

• Meanwhile make the puffs. Preheat the oven to 200 ºC/400 ºF.

• In a saucepan bring milk slowly to the boil with the butter and when the butter has melted add all the flour at once. Stir until the mixture forms a pastry ball and leaves the sides of the pan .Turn off the heat. Allow the pastry ball to cool and stir in the egg and cheese.

• Transfer the pastry to a pastry bag with a small, smooth nozzle and squeeze onto a lightly greased or lined baking sheet, making small mounds about 1 inch apart.

• Bake the cheese puffs for 5-6 minutes until they have doubled in size and are golden brown.

To serve. Puree the soup with a mixer or food processor. Stir in the cream and season the soup with nutmeg, salt and freshly ground pepper.

• Ladle the soup into warmed deep bowls and garnish with the cheese puffs. Garnish with small cauliflower florets and parsley.

Erwtensoep: Pea soup

400 g/10 oz green split peas
$^1/_2$ celeriac
1 small carrot
100 g/3$^1/_2$ oz smoked bacon,
cut into pieces
400 g/14 oz pork chump chops
200 g/7 oz leeks, sliced
$^1/_2$ bunch fresh celery leaves
$^1/_2$ bunch parsley
250 g/8 oz smoked pork sausage
salt and freshly ground pepper

Preparation/serving: approx.
1$^3/_4$ hours/10 minutes
Contains per serving: 792 kJ/533 kcal.
53 g protein, 43 g fat, 47 g carbo-
hydrate

Preparation. Wash the split peas. Peel and dice the celeriac and carrot. Cover the peas, vegetables, smoked bacon and chump chops with 1$^1/_2$ litres/ 3 pints water and bring to the boil. Simmer for 1$^1/_2$ hours until meat is tender. Add leeks 15 minutes before serving.

• Meanwhile finely chop the celery leaves and parsley and slice the smoked sausage. Remove the chops from the soup and remove meat from the bones.

To serve. Return meat to the pan. Add the herbs, smoked sausage, salt and pepper to taste and simmer for 10 more minutes, stirring occasionally.

• Delicious with black bread spread with coarse mustard and a layer of smoked bacon.

• Traditionally pigs trotters were cooked with the soup, but while these are no longer widely available certain butchers may still have them.

Variation

If vegetables al dente are preferred, only cook the celeriac and carrot for about 20 minutes and stir in the chopped celery leaves just before serving. The soup can be made lighter and creamier by substituting $^1/_2$ litre milk for $^1/_2$ litre water.

Hearty chicken soup

1 onion
1 leek
1 large carrot
2 celery sticks
1 red pepper
1 bunch spring onions
1 boiling chicken
1 bouquet garni: sprigs thyme,
parsley and bay leaf tied
together
4 white peppercorns
1 small piece nutmeg
50 g/2 oz vermicelli
100 g/3$^{1}/_{2}$ oz sweetcorn (tin)
1 tablespoon finely chopped
celery
salt and freshly ground pepper

Preparation/serving: approx.
45 minutes/5 minutes
Allowing to cool: about 2-3 hours
Contains per serving: 913 kJ/217 kcal.
26 g protein, 8 g fat, 11 g carbohydrate

Tip
Remove the skin and fat from the
chicken beforehand if the soup is to
be eaten on the same day.

Preparation. Peel and chop the onion. Slice the leek in rings and dice the carrot and celery sticks. Cut the red pepper into pieces and the spring onions into rings.

• Place the chicken in a large saucepan and cover with 1$^{1}/_{2}$ litre/3 pints cold water. Bring the water to the boil and remove the floating scum with a skimmer. Repeat again.

• Add the vegetables, bouquet garni, peppercorns and nutmeg to the chicken and simmer everything for about 1$^{1}/_{2}$ hours until chicken is tender.

• Remove the chicken from the stock, allow to cool slightly and remove meat from the bones. Cut the chicken into small pieces. Strain the stock into a clean pan and season to taste. Allow the stock 2-3 hours to cool and skim off any congealed fat.

To serve. Heat the stock and add the chicken, pepper, spring onions and vermicelli. Heat through over a low heat for about three minutes, then stir in the sweetcorn and chopped celery. Adjust seasoning.

• Delicious with thinly sliced crepes.

Variation
Add a small can of cocoanut milk, 1 chilli pepper and 100 g/3$^{1}/_{2}$ oz
peeled prawns.

Bruinebonensoep: Bean soup

350 g/12 oz dried butter beans
salt and freshly ground pepper
2 large potatoes
2 bay leaves
6 peppercorns
3 cloves
3 onions
50 g/2 oz butter
$1/2$ teaspoon curry powder
3 tablespoons finely chopped parsley
2 tablespoons Worcester sauce

*Preparation/cooking: approx.
10 minutes/1$1/2$ hours
Soaking: 12 hours
Contains per serving: 1610 kJ/382 kcal.
19 g protein, 12 g fat, 50 g carbohydrate*

Preparation. Soak the beans in 1$1/2$ litres/3 pints water for 12 hours with a pinch of salt.
• Peel, wash and cut the potatoes into pieces. Bring the beans in their water to the boil, adding bay leaves, peppercorns and cloves. Simmer for about 1-1$1/2$ hours. Add the potatoes half an hour before the cooking time is up.
• Meanwhile peel and finely chopped the onions. Heat the butter, fry the onion, add the curry powder and continue frying a few minutes more.
To serve. Remove the bay leaves, cloves and peppercorns from the pan and puree the beans and potatoes in the cooking liquid with a hand blender. Stir in the onions and simmer the soup for another 10 minutes until nicely blended. Add the parsley and season the soup with salt, freshly ground pepper and Worcester sauce.

Variations
* Add small meat balls to the soup and simmer for 10 minutes until cooked.
* Enrich the flavour of the soup by frying a finely chopped chilli pepper and 2 cloves garlic with the onions. Add 1 diced red pepper, 8 cherry tomatoes, halved, and substitute chives for the parsley. Sprinkle a generous spoonful of mature cheese over each bowl of soup and serve immediately.

LIGHT SOUPS

Koninginnesoep: Queen's soup

1 litre/2 pints chicken stock
30 g/1 oz flour
150 g/5 oz smoked salmon, in
pieces
freshly ground pepper
pinch nutmeg
few drops lemon juice
1 egg yolk
100 ml/3^1/$_2$ fl oz cream
2 tablespoons finely chopped
dill

Preparation/serving: approx. 25 minutes
Contains per serving: 1095 kJ/264 kcal.
12 g protein, 21 g fat, 7 g carbohydrate

Preparation. Heat the chicken stock. Melt the butter in a large saucepan and stir in the flour. Pour the stock into the cooked flour, stirring all the while, and simmer gently for about 10 minutes.
• Season the soup with pepper, nutmeg and lemon juice.
To serve. Beat the egg yolk with the cream and stir in 5 tablespoons of the hot soup. Remove the pan from the heat and stir the mixture through the soup.
• Serve the soup in deep plates or bowls and sprinkle with salmon and dill.

Variation
Substitute 300 g/10 oz chicken cubes for the salmon and heat through in the soup. Garnish with fresh chives instead of dill.

Cream of tomato soup

1 kilo/2 lb tomatoes
2 onions
2 cloves garlic
^{1}/$_2$ litre/1 pint veal or chicken
stock (tub)
2 tablespoons finely chopped
thyme
1 small tub crème fraîche
salt and freshly ground pepper
1 tablespoon finely chopped
fresh herbs

Preparation. Wash the tomatoes and cut in two. Peel and finely chop the onion and garlic.
• In a large pan bring the stock, tomatoes, garlic and thyme to the boil and simmer for 20 minutes.
To serve. Puree the soup in a food processor or with a masher and stir in the crème fraîche. Season to taste with salt, pepper and fresh herbs.
• Delicious with crispy cheese straws.

Preparation/cooking: approx. 30 minutes
Contains per serving: 620 kJ/149 kcal.
3 g protein, 11 g fat, 10 g carbohydrate

Limburg asparagus soup with ham-off-the-bone and egg mimosa

300 g/10 oz white asparagus
3/4 litre/1 1/2 pints vegetable stock (tub)
1 teaspoon sugar
30 g/1 oz butter
30 g/1 oz flour
100 ml/3 1/2 fl oz cream
pinch grated nutmeg
salt and freshly ground pepper
200 g/7 oz ham-off-the-bone
3 eggs, hardboiled
1 tablespoon finely chopped parsley

Preparation/serving: approx. 40/5 minutes

Contains per serving: 1324 kJ/318 kcal.
16 g protein, 24 g fat, 9 g carbohydrate

Variation
Substitute small pieces of fresh salmon for the ham and heat through. Garnish with fresh dill instead of parsley.

Preparation. Peel the asparagus with a paring knife, removing the tough ends. Remove the tips (about 3 cm/1 in) and cook in a little vegetable stock for about 10 minutes until tender. Drain and put aside for later.

• Cut the remaining asparagus into 3 cm/1 in pieces and cook in the stock with the sugar for 15-20 minutes until tender. Puree the asparagus and stock in a food processor or using a masher until a smooth soup.

• Melt the butter in a large pan and stir in the flour. Cook gently for 2 minutes and add the soup and cream. Bring slowly to the boil and simmer for about 3 minutes. Season with salt, pepper and nutmeg.

To serve. Dice the ham. Peel the eggs and press through a sieve. Divide the ham and asparagus tips among the four soup bowls.

• Ladle the soup into the bowls and garnish with egg mimosa and parsley.

Hutspot: Carrot and potato mash

MASHED DISHES AND OTHER ONE-PAN MEALS

400 g/14 oz marbled braising
steak
4 onions
75 g/3 oz butter
2 bay leaves
1 teaspoon dill seeds or
1 tablespoon fresh dill
salt and freshly ground pepper
750 g/1¹/2 lb potatoes
750 g/1¹/2 lb carrots

*Preparation/serving: approx.
2¹/2 hours/5 minutes
Contains per serving: 2031 kJ/ 486 kcal.
25 g protein, 28 g fat, 34 g carbohydrate*

Preparation. Cut the meat into cubes. Peel and
slice 2 onions.
• Heat the butter in a large casserole. Fry the meat
on all sides over a high heat until brown. Add the
onions and continue frying.
• Add a little water, bay leaves, dill, salt and pepper,
then cover and simmer for 2 hours until meat is
tender.
• Peel and cut the potatoes into pieces. Wash the
carrots and slice the remaining onions into rings.
Cook the vegetables in a little water and salt for
about 25 minutes until tender.
To serve. Drain and finely mash the vegetables.
• Add the braised meat and some of the gravy to
the vegetables and mix until a smooth thick
'stamppot'. Season to taste and serve the remaining gravy separately.

Variation
*Spicy hutspot. Substitute 1 teaspoon cardamom powder and 1 tea-
spoon coriander powder for the dill. Delicious with finely chopped
onions fried golden brown.*

4 SERVINGS

500 g/1 lb eating apples
(Elstar)
500 g/1 lb cooking apples
1 kg/2 lb potatoes
25 g/1 oz butter
300 g/10 oz minced beef and
pork
salt and freshly ground pepper
300 g/10 oz chunk smoked
bacon
50 ml/2 fl oz milk
pinch all spice
pinch cinnamon

*Preparation/cooking: approx.
40 minutes*

*Contains per serving: 3210 kJ/769 kcal.
31 g protein, 45 g fat, 59 g carbohydrate*

Variation
*Substitute 250 g/8 oz chicken liver
for the mince. Season to taste with
salt and pepper and 1 teaspoon
chilli sauce. Serve separately with
the mash mixture ('stamppot').*

Preparation. Peel, core and chop the apples. Peel the potatoes and cut into pieces.

• Heat the butter in a pan and stir-fry the mince until brown and tender. Season to taste and put aside until later.

• Put the potatoes in a large pan and just cover with water. Arrange the apples over the potatoes and place the piece of smoked bacon on top. Simmer partly covered for about 25 minutes until bacon is tender.

• Drain and remove bacon from the pan. Cut up bacon into small cubes.

• Heat the milk with the all-spice and cinnamon.

To serve. Using the spicy hot milk, mash the potato and apple together until well-blended and creamy. Add the mince and bacon cubes and serve immediately.

MASHED DISHES AND OTHER ONE-PAN MEALS

White bean and carrot stew

2 shallots
3 cloves garlic
2 large carrots
1 red pepper
1 large pot white beans
(700 g/1^1/$_2$ lb)
50 g/2 oz butter
600 g/20 oz stewing beef
salt and freshly ground pepper
200 ml/7 fl oz beef stock
(carton)
1 teaspoon paprika powder
1 small tin tomato puree

*Preparation/serving: approx.
1^1/$_2$ hours/30 minutes
Contains per serving: 1728 kJ/411 kcal.
43 g protein, 15 g fat, 25 g carbohydrate*

Preparation. Peel and finely chop the shallots and garlic clove. Wash and dice the carrots. De-seed and slice the pepper. Rinse the beans under cold running water and drain in a sieve.

• Heat the butter in a casserole and brown the meat all over. Add the shallots and garlic and continue frying over a high heat. Season with salt and pepper.

• Pour in the stock and leave the meat to simmer over a low heat for 1-1^1/$_2$ hours until tender.

To serve. Add the paprika powder, carrot, pepper, white beans and tomato puree to the meat and cook gently for a further 20 minutes. Add more stock if needed. Serve on a warmed platter.

• Delicious with a crisp mixed salad with cherry tomatoes.

Variation

Substitute stewing lamb for beef and mild curry powder for the paprika powder mixed with 1 tablespoon cumin. Omit the red pepper and add 100 ml/3^1/$_2$ fl oz yoghurt and finely chopped mint towards the end of the cooking time. Garnish with roasted white almonds.

Filosoof: Dutch Shepherd's pie

1 onion
750 g/1½ lb potatoes
50 g/2 oz butter
500 g/1lb minced beef
200 ml/7 fl oz beef stock
150 ml/5 fl oz milk
2 teaspoons cornflour
salt and freshly ground pepper
1 teaspoon mixed fresh herbs
½ teaspoon nutmeg
25 g/1 oz breadcrumbs
25 g/1oz mature Gouda cheese
or any mature cheese, grated
15 g/½ oz chilled butter

*Preparation/cooking: approx.
35/25 minutes*

*Contains per serving: 2484kJ/596 kcal.
31 g protein, 38 g fat, 33 g carbohydrate*

Preparation. Peel the potatoes and cut into pieces. Cook for about 20 minutes in just enough water to cover.

• Meanwhile peel and finely chop the onion. Heat 25 g/1 oz butter in a frying pan and brown the mince all over. Add the onion and fry for a further 5 minutes. Pour on the stock and leave to simmer for 10 minutes.

• Heat the milk in a saucepan. Drain the potatoes and mash with the milk and remaining butter.

• Mix the cornflour with a little water, then while stirring add the mixture to the mince. Season to taste with salt and fresh herbs. Season the puree to taste with salt, pepper and nutmeg.

• Lightly grease an oven dish and heat the oven to 200 °C/400 °F.

Cooking. Divide half the puree over the base of the oven dish. Over this arrange the mince and then the rest of the potato puree. Sprinkle with breadcrumbs and cheese and dot with butter. Bake the shepherd's pie in the oven for 25 minutes until the top is crisp and golden brown.

• Delicious with a mixed salad.

Variation
*Italian shepherd's pie. Mix segments of
sundried tomato, 2 finely chopped cloves of
garlic and finely chopped basil into the mince.
Bake in olive oil rather than butter and
for the topping use grated Parmesan
and breadcrumbs.*

4 SERVINGS

Zuurkoolstamppot: Sauerkraut 'stamppot'

1¹/₂ kilo/3 lb potatoes
600 g/20 oz sauerkraut
salt and freshly ground pepper
1 bay leaf
2 onions
50 g/2 oz butter
100 g/3¹/₂ oz piece lean smoked bacon
4 pork sausages
2 tablespoons flour

*Preparation/serving: approx.
1 hour/10 minutes
Contains per serving: 3039 kJ/727 kcal.
29 g protein, 42 g fat, 58 g carbohydrate*

Variation

*Add 1 tablespoon curry powder to
the onion and stir 100 g/3¹/₂ oz
raisins into the 'stamppot'. Arrange
layers in a lightly greased oven
dish, alternating with layers of
sliced sautéed chicken breast. Top
with breadcrumbs and dots of butter and bake in a preheated oven
at 200 ºC/400 ºF until
golden brown.*

Preparation. Peel the potatoes and cut into pieces.
Bring the potatoes and sauerkraut to the boil in
just enough water to cover the bottom of the pan.
Add a bay leaf and cook for about 25 – 30 minutes
until done
• Meanwhile peel and slice the onions into rings.
Heat half the butter in a frying pan and fry the
onions over a low heat for 15 minutes until brown
and crispy. Dice the bacon and fry until brown and
crispy.
• Roll the sausages through the flour. Heat the
remaining butter in a casserole and fry the sausages, turning occasionally. Add a little water and
braise them for 20 minutes until cooked.
To serve. Drain the sauerkraut and save the
cooking liquid. Mash the sauerkraut and potato
together and stir in the fried onion, diced bacon
and bacon fat. More cooking liquid can be added
to make the 'stamppot' smoother.
Adjust seasoning. Remove the sausages
from the cooking juices and reduce
liquid over a high heat.
• Serve the sauerkraut with
sausage and the sauce.
• Delicious with fried pineapple
slices.

Boerenkoolstamppot: Curly kale 'stamppot'

4 SERVINGS

1¹/2 kilo/3 lb potatoes
2 onions
1 bay leaf
600 g/20 oz curly kale, stalks
removed and finely chopped
salt and freshly ground pepper
1 smoked sausage
(350 g/12 oz)
150 ml/5 fl oz milk
25 g/1 oz butter

Preparation/serving: approx.
40 minutes/5 minutes
Contains per serving: 2648 kJ/632 kcal.
26 g protein, 32 g fat, 59 g carbo-
hydrate

Preparation. Peel the potatoes and cut into pieces.
Peel and slice the onions.
• Put the potatoes, curly kale, onion and bay leaf
with seasoning in a large pan. Add just enough
water to cover the bottom of the pan and cook
over a low heat for about 25 minutes until cooked.
• Meanwhile simmer the sausage in its sealed
wrapper for about 25 minutes.
• Remove the bay leaf from the pan, drain the
vegetables and mash finely.
Heat the milk and butter and stir through the
potato and curly kale mash until smooth. Adjust
the 'stamppot' for seasoning.
To serve. Remove the sausage from the wrapper,
slice into pieces and arrange over the 'stamppot'.
Delicious with coarse mustard, brown sauce and
fried bacon rashers.

Variation
Use sour cream instead of milk to enrich the mash. Serve with sautéed
cubes of chorizo and slices of roasted red pepper.

Endive 'stamppot' with mushrooms and cheese

1¹/₂ kilo/3 lb potatoes
salt and freshly ground pepper
50 g/2 oz butter
200 g/7 oz chunk smoked bacon, diced
250 g/8 oz mushrooms
150 ml/6 fl oz milk
600 g/20 oz endive, finely sliced
nutmeg
200 g/7 oz mature Dutch cumin cheese (or any full-flavoured cheese with cumin)

Preparation/serving: approx. 50 minutes

Contains per serving: 3103 kJ/743 kcal. 31 g protein, 45 g fat, 54 g carbohydrate

Preparation. Peel the potatoes and cut into pieces. Cook for about 20-25 minutes in just enough water to cover.

• Meanwhile heat the butter in a frying pan and fry the bacon pieces. Clean and slice the mushrooms. Add these to the bacon and continue frying.

• Heat the milk in a saucepan. Drain the potatoes and mash with the hot milk until smooth.

• Mix the endive, bacon and mushroom mixture, pepper and nutmeg into the potato puree and heat through again.

To serve. Cut the cheese into small pieces and mix into the 'stamppot'. Serve immediately.

Variation
Substitute turnip greens or Swiss chard for the endive and stir cubes of blue cheese through the 'stamppot'.

Chickpeas with apple salad

2 tins chick peas (1 large,
1 small)
2 Bramley apples
50 ml/2 fl oz apple juice
50 g/2 oz raisins
25 g/1 oz butter
200 g/7 oz bacon, diced
2 large onions
pepper

*Preparation/serving: approx.
20/10 minutes*

*Contains per serving: 2035 kJ/486 kcal.
21 g protein, 26 g fat, 43 g carbohydrate*

Preparation. Drain the chickpeas and rinse under cold running water.
• Peel, core and roughly chop the apples. Mix in a bowl with the apple juice and raisins. Leave a little while to marinate.
• Heat the butter in a large pan and fry the diced bacon until crisp. Peel and finely chop the onion. Add to the diced bacon and continue frying for a further 10 minutes.
To serve. Stir the chickpeas into the bacon and onions and leave to heat through for about 10 minutes. Season to taste and serve with an apple salad.
• Delicious with sautéed potatoes.

Variation
*To accompany the chickpeas have small bowls of diced red pepper,
tomato and slithers of raw onion on the table.*

MASHED DISHES AND OTHER ONE-PAN MEALS

Baked spinach with tomato and minced veal

Potato puree for 4 people (see
p. 54)
2 red onions
1 kg/2 lb spinach
4 beef tomatoes
25 g/1oz butter
500 g/1 lb minced veal
1 tablespoon finely chopped
rosemary
2 tablespoons tomato puree
salt and cayenne pepper
100 g/3¹/2 oz fresh cream
cheese
50 g/2 oz breadcrumbs

*Preparation/cooking: approx.
10/25 minutes*

*Contains per serving: 2978 kJ/712 kcal.
41 g protein, 38 g fat, 51 g carbohydrate*

Preparation. Preheat the oven to 200 °C/400 °F.
Peel and slice the onion into rings. Wash the spinach and thickly slice the tomatoes.
• Heat the butter in a large pan and brown the
minced veal all over. Add the onions, rosemary and
tomato puree and sauté everything for a further
3 minutes. Stir the spinach into the veal a little at
a time and fry quickly over a high heat. Season to
taste with salt and cayenne pepper.
Cooking. Arrange half the potato puree in a lightly
greased casserole and evenly cover with the veal
mixture. Arrange the sliced tomatoes on top and
cover with the remaining potato puree.
• Top with an even layer of cream cheese and then
the breadcrumbs. Bake in the oven for about
25 minutes until crisp and golden brown.

Creamy ragout of veal with parsley rice

400 g/14 oz veal steak
1 onion
50 g/2 oz butter
500 m/17 fl oz veal stock
1 bouquet garni comprising
2 sprigs thyme, 2 springs parsley and a bay leaf
salt and freshly ground pepper
300 g/10 oz rice
40 g/1^1/2 flour
150 m/5 fl oz cream
squeeze of lemon juice
pinch of nutmeg
2 tablespoons finely chopped parsley

Preparation/cooking: approx. 1^1/2 hours

Contains per serving: 2792 kJ/666 kcal. 30 g protein, 29 g fat, 71 g carbohydrate

Variation

Ragout of veal with wild mushrooms. Slice 250g/8 oz of cultivated or mixed wild mushrooms. Sauté these in a knob of butter in a frying pan over a high heat with a few sprigs of fresh thyme until brown. Add at the last minute to the ragout of veal.

Preparation. The veal should be at room temperature before cutting in small pieces. Peel and finely chop the onion.

• Melt 10 g/^{1}/2 oz butter in a medium sized saucepan and fry the onion until translucent. Stir in the veal and add the hot stock, bouquet garni and seasoning. Return to the boil, cover the pan and simmer over a low heat for 1 hour until meat is tender.

• Cook the rice according to instructions on packet.

• Melt the remaining butter in a heavy-bottomed saucepan. Stir in the flour and add the cooking liquid from the veal. Continue stirring until the sauce is thoroughly blended.

• Add the veal and cream. Simmer the ragout for about 10 minutes and adjust the seasoning with a few drops of lemon juice, salt, pepper and nutmeg. Stir the parsley into the rice.

To serve. Lightly oil a timbale or small cup and pile the rice into the mould, pressing it down well. Reverse onto a warmed dish. Arrange the ragout around the rice and serve at once.

Eggs in herbal and mustard sauce

8 eggs
50 g/2 oz butter
50 g/2 oz flour
$^1/_2$ litre/1 pint milk
1 herb or vegetarian
stock cube
2-3 tablespoons soft mustard
2 tablespoons finely
chopped parsley
2 tablespoons finely
chopped chives
salt and freshly ground pepper

*Preparation/serving: approx.
20 minutes*

*Contains per serving: 1455 kJ/349 kcal.
19 g protein, 23 g fat, 16 g carbohydrate*

Variation
*Substitute finely chopped tarragon
or basil for the parsley and serve
with a tomato salad.*

Preparation. Boil the eggs for about 8 minutes until hard. Meanwhile melt the butter in a pan and stir in the flour until smooth. Pour in the milk, while stirring, and bring to the boil. Continue stirring until the liquid and flour has blended.

• Crumble the stock cube into the sauce and add the mustard. Leave the sauce to simmer gently for about 8 minutes until it thickens.

• Plunge the eggs in cold water and peel. Halve the eggs lengthwise and place, white side up, in a shallow dish.

• Stir the chopped herbs into the sauce and add seasoning to taste.

To serve. Spoon the sauce over the eggs.

• Delicious with puréed potato or junks of wholemeal bread and a fresh cucumber salad.

Pan-fried cheese slices with spicy apple compote

3 firm apples
50 ml/2 fl oz apple juice
2 spring onions
2 tablespoons ginger jam
2 teaspoons hot chilli sauce
salt and freshly ground pepper
300 g/10 oz mild Gouda or mild Cheddar cheese
2 eggs
100 g/3^1/$_2$ oz breadcrumbs
50 g/2 oz butter

Preparation/cooking: approx. 30 minutes

Contains per serving: 2337 kJ/561 kcal. 25 g protein, 37 g fat, 32 g carbo-hydrate

Variations
* Make a spicy coating by mixing 1 tablespoon curry powder, kebab or taco spices into the breadcrumbs.

Preparation. Peel, core and chop the apples into small pieces. Bring the apple juice and pieces of apple in a pan to the boil and cook for about 5 minutes until just tender and the liquid has evaporated.

• Slice the spring onions into thin rings and mix through the apple with the ginger jam and chilli sauce. Add salt and pepper to taste. Refrigerate the compote until ready to use.

• Remove rind from the cheese and cut into 4 or 8 equal slices, about 2 cm/^{3}/$_4$ in thick. Beat the eggs in a deep plate. Roll the slices of cheese in the egg and then in the breadcrumbs. Repeat, pressing the breadcrumbs down well.

• Heat the butter in a frying pan and quickly sauté the sliced cheese over a high heat for about 4 minutes until nicely brown, turning once. The cheese slices are done just before they start to spread out in the pan.

To serve. Serve the cheese slices with spoonfuls of apple compote. Delicious with small boiled new potatoes and a salad.

Braised cod with tomato, lemon and parsley

600 g/20 oz thick cod fillet
salt and freshly ground pepper
2 tomatoes
3 spring onions or one
small leek
1 small bunch parsley
1 lemon
75 g/3 oz butter

*Preparation/cooking: approx.
20 minutes*

*Contains per serving: 1145 kJ/274 kcal.
28 g protein, 17 g fat, 3 g carbohydrate*

Variations

* Braise the cod in 100 ml/4 fl oz
white wine.
* Lay the cod and other ingredients
in a greased oven dish. Sprinkle
over a handful of breadcrumbs, and
dot with the remaining butter. Bake
in a preheated oven at 200 ºC/400
ºF for 20 minutes until golden
brown and cooked.

Preparation. Blot the cod dry with paper towel; cut into four equal fillets and season well.
• Peel the tomatoes: score the skins, plunge into boiling water for 30 seconds and lift off the skins. Drain, de-seed and chop the tomatoes.
• Wash the spring onions (or leek) and slice thinly. Finely chop the parsley. Cut four slices of lemon. Squeeze the juice from the remaining lemon.
• Melt 50 g/2 oz of butter in a frying pan and add the cod fillets. Sprinkle over the onions and parsley. Sprinkle the lemon juice on top and place a slice of lemon and some chopped tomato onto each fillet. Season well and dot the remaining butter over the fish.
• Cover with a lid and braise the cod fillets over a low heat for 8 minutes until done.
To serve. Place the fillets with the parsley and spring onions on four warmed plates. Reduce the liquid in the pan by cooking over a high heat for 2 minutes and pour over the fish.
• Delicious with mange-tout and baby new potatoes in their jackets.

Steamed mussels with herb sauce

1 leek
2 small carrots
1 clove garlic
2 kg/4 1b mussels
50 g/2 oz butter
2 sprigs thyme
For the herb sauce:
1/2 small bunch parsley
1/2 small bunch chives
1/2 small bunch chervil
1/2 tsp cornflour
125 ml/5 fl oz crème fraîche
freshly ground pepper

*Preparation/cooking: approx.
25 minutes*

*Contains per serving: 2817 kJ/679 kcal.
28 g protein, 53 g fat, 22 g carbohydrate*

Variation
*Fried mussels. Remove steamed
mussels from the shells, toss in
flour and fry over a medium heat
for 4 minutes until brown. Delicious
as an appetizer or as a light lunch
with a mustard or tomato sauce.*

Preparation. Clean the leek and carrots. Cut the leeks into thin rings and slice the carrots. Peel and chop the garlic into small pieces.

• Scrub the mussels thoroughly under cold running water, discarding cracked mussels or open ones that don't close again when tapped against the work surface.

• **Cooking.** Melt the butter in a large heavy-bottomed saucepan. Add the mussels, then strew the leek, carrots, garlic, thyme and a sprig of parsley on top. Cook the mussels in their own steam over a high heat for 8 minutes, or until they have all opened (shake the pan a few times during cooking so that the mussels readily open).

• Finely chop the parsley, chives and chervil.

• Pile the mussels and vegetables into a deep pre-heated bowl and keep warm. Boil 100 ml/4 fl oz of the cooking liquid in the saucepan until it is reduced to a third. Stir the cornflour into the crème fraîche, then, while stirring, add to the mussel liquid. Continue stirring until thoroughly blended. Leave the sauce to simmer gently for about 2 minutes and stir in the finely chopped herbs. Add pepper to taste.

To serve. Spoon the hot herb sauce over the mussels or serve separately. Delicious with French fries and a mixed green and tomato salad.

2 SERVINGS

Fried plaice with almonds

50 g/2 oz flour
2 plaices
salt and freshly ground pepper
1 teaspoon paprika powder
1 orange
75 ml (3 fl oz) medium dry
sherry
50 g/2 oz butter
50 g/2 oz flaked almonds
1 tablespoon finely chopped
chives

Preparation/cooking: approx. 20 minutes
Contains per serving: 2308 kJ/555 kcal.
36 g protein, 36 g fat, 12 g carbo-
hydrate

Variation
Substitute thinly sliced chestnut
mushrooms for the almonds. Sauté
the mushrooms in butter over a
high heat until brown and until the
liquid evaporates. Add chives and
seasoning to taste.

Preparation. Sprinkle the flour onto a plate. Blot the plaice dry with paper towel. Rub the plaice with the salt, pepper and paprika powder and dip in the flour, shaking off surplus.

• Heat the butter in a large frying pan and fry the plaice over a medium heat for 8-10 minutes until golden brown and cooked. Turn half way through cooking.

• Meanwhile squeeze the juice from the orange.

• Lay the plaice on 2 warmed plates and cover with foil to keep warm. Stir the orange juice and sherry into the cooking juices and boil down rapidly for 2 minutes.

To serve. Roast the flaked almonds in a dry frying pan until golden brown and sprinkle the chives over the plaice. Serve the sauce separately.

• Delicious with saffron rice and garden peas.

MEAT AND GAME DISHES

500 g/1 lb broccoli
salt and freshly ground pepper
1 large red onion
1 yellow pepper
25 g/1 oz butter
1 lemon
300 g/10 oz cod fillet
300 g/10 oz salmon fillet
100 g/4 oz cream cheese
100 ml/4 fl oz single cream
1/2 tablespoon fresh thyme
leaves
pinch nutmeg
100 g/4 oz cooked mussels
100 g/4 oz prawns
50 g/2 oz mature Gouda cheese
or any mature cheese, grated

*Preparation/cooking: approx.
25/25 minutes*

*Contains per serving: 2455 kJ/590 kcal.
50 g protein, 41 g fat, 5 g carbohydrate*

Preparation. Preheat the oven to 200 °C/400 °F. Cut the broccoli from the stalk in flowerets and place in boiling, salted water for around 3 minutes until just tender. Drain in a colander. Finely slice the onion and pepper (de-seeded) in small pieces.

• Melt the butter in a pan, stir in the onion and pepper and cook gently for about 5 minutes. Wash the lemon and finely grate the rind. Squeeze out the lemon juice.

• Cut the cod and salmon fillet into 3 cm (1 in) pieces and sprinkle with lemon juice.

• In a large bowl mix the cream cheese with the cream, thyme, salt, pepper, grated rind and pinch of nutmeg. Stir in the broccoli, cod, salmon, mussels, shrimps and onion and pepper mixture. Turn into a shallow baking dish.

Cooking. Sprinkle the grated cheese over the mixture and bake in the oven for around 25 minutes until golden brown and cooked.

• Delicious with mashed potatoes and a grated carrot and parsley salad.

Variation
Fennel can be substituted for the broccoli and nutmeg. Add Pernod to the sauce, according to taste, and garnish with fennel leaves.

Beef roll-ups stuffed with mince, bacon and gherkins

1 slice old bread
a little milk
200 g/7 oz minced beef and pork
salt and freshly ground pepper
nutmeg
4 slices of stewing or uncooked roast beef (total weight 400 g/14 oz) beaten as thin as possible
4 bacon rashers
4 gherkins
cocktail sticks
25 g/10z butter
50 ml/2 fl oz beef stock
100 ml/3¹/2 fl oz buttermilk

Preparation/cooking: approx. 15/30 minutes

Contains per serving: 1392 kJ/334 kcal. 34 g protein, 20 g fat, 3 g carbohydrate

Preparation. Remove the crusts from the bread and soak in the milk. Combine the mince with the bread and add salt, pepper and nutmeg to taste.

• Distribute the mince evenly between the pieces of beef. Place a bacon rasher and a gherkin on the mince and roll up the slices of beef. Secure with a toothpick.

• Heat the butter in a large casserole and carefully sear the beef roll-ups all over. Sprinkle with salt and pepper.

• Add the heated stock, cover and leave the meat to cook gently for about 30-40 minutes until tender.

To serve. Remove the beef roll-ups from the dish and remove toothpicks.

• Stir the buttermilk into the broth and serve separately with the meat.

• Delicious with potato puree, green beans and a cucumber salad.

Variation
Stuff the beef slices with mince seasoned with garlic, thyme, pine nuts and finely chopped black olives. Substitute cream for buttermilk.

Spicy-coated roast chicken

1,200 g/2^{1}/$_{2}$ 1b free-range chicken
1 lemon
salt and freshly ground pepper
4 springs fresh thyme
50 g/2 oz butter
1 tablespoon curry powder
100 ml/4 fl oz white wine

Preparation/cooking: approx.
1^{1}/$_{2}$ hours
Contains per serving: 1112 kJ/ 268 kcal.
18 g protein, 19 g fat, 0 g carbohydrate

Variation
Stuff the chicken with a mixture of fried onions, mushrooms, garlic and a handful of finely chopped hazelnuts.

Preparation. Chicken should be at room temperature. Preheat the oven to 200 ºC/400 ºF. Slice half the lemon, and squeeze the juice from the other half. Blot the chicken dry with paper towel and rub the chicken inside with salt and pepper. Stuff the bird with the lemon slices, sprigs of thyme and 25 g/1 oz butter. Close the cavity with a toothpick.
• Melt the remaining butter in a small saucepan and add the chilli powder, curry powder and salt and pepper to taste. Brush the chicken with the spicy butter and bind the legs together. Transfer the chicken to a roasting tin and place on a rack in the middle of the oven.
• Roast the chicken for around 1-1^{1}/$_{2}$ hrs until golden brown and tender. Frequently baste with the cooking juices. Cover the chicken with foil if it becomes too brown. Remove the chicken from the oven and leave to rest for 5 minutes.
• Add the lemon juice and white wine to the juices in the roasting tin and boil rapidly over a high heat to reduce to a thin sauce.
To serve. Bring the chicken to the table and carve. Serve the sauce separately.
• Delicious with broccoli and pan-fried potatoes.

4 SERVINGS

Meat stew with cranberry compote

MEAT AND GAME DISHES

750 g/1¹/₂ pound stewing beef
3 onions
100 g/3¹/₂ oz butter
salt and freshly ground pepper
250 ml/10 fl oz beef stock
2 bay leaves
2 cloves
1 teaspoon juniper berries
2 sprigs rosemary
2 tablespoons vinegar
For the compote
450 g/1 lb cranberries
200 ml/7 fl oz orange juice
50 g/2 oz sugar

Preparation/serving: approx.
3 hours/20 minutes
Contains per serving: 2394 kJ/574 kcal.
40 g protein, 36 g fat, 21 g carbohydrate

Preparation. Blot the stewing beef dry with paper-towel. Peel and finely chop 1 onion.
• Heat half the butter in a casserole and brown the meat all over. Season with salt and pepper, add the onion and fry for a further 2 minutes.
• Heat the stock and pour over the meat. Add the bay leaves, cloves, juniper berries, rosemary and vinegar and bring to the boil. Cover, and leave to simmer over a low heat for 2¹/₂ - 3 hours until meat is tender.
• Meanwhile make the cranberry compote. Bring cranberries, orange juice and sugar to the boil. Stir continuously until berries open and leave to cool.
To serve. Peel and finely slice the remaining onions into rings.
• Heat the remaining butter in a pan and fry the onion rings for about 3 minutes until translucent.
• Serve the stewing beef with the onion rings and cranberry compote.

Variations
* Stew the beef in beer and serve with fried bacon rashers and mushrooms.
* You can also replace half the stock with red wine, but then omit the vinegar.

Meatballs with bacon and rosemary

1 onion
2 cloves garlic
75 g/3 oz butter
100 g/3^1/$_2$ oz piece smoked
bacon, diced
2 teaspoons finely chopped
rosemary
2 slices stale white bread
100 ml/3^1/$_2$ fl oz milk
1 egg
500 g/1 lb beef and pork mince
salt and pepper
breadcrumbs

Preparation/cooking: approx.
1^1/$_2$ hours

Contains per serving: 2726 kJ/657 kcal.
30 g protein, 53 g fat, 15 g carbo-
hydrate

Variation
Spicy meatballs. Add 1 teaspoon
hot chilli sauce to the mince and
stir 1 tablespoon sweet soy sauce
through the gravy. Leave ont the
rosemary.

Preparation. Peel the onion and garlic. Finely chop the onion and garlic.
• Heat half the butter in a frying pan and fry the diced bacon. Add the onion and garlic and sauté until translucent Add the rosemary and fry for about three more minutes.
• Trim the crusts from the bread and soak in milk. Squeeze the bread out and mix this through the bacon mixture and the egg through the mince. Season the mince to taste and shape into 8 balls. Roll these through the breadcrumbs.
• Heat the rest of the butter in a large casserole and sauté the meatballs until brown on all sides. Reduce heat and cook for about 20 minutes, partly covered with a lid, until done. Turn occasionally.
To serve. Remove meatballs from the pan and add a little water to the cooking juices. Scrap up the coagulated juices of the pan and reduce the liquid on a high heat.
• Delicious with potato puree and a carrot and celeriac salad (make a dressing from 1 tablespoon vinegar, ^{1}/$_2$ pint sour cream, 3 tablespoons mayonnaise, 1 tablespoon soft mustard and 1 tablespoon finely chopped parsley).

4 SERVINGS

Braised rabbit in mustard cream

4 rabbit quarters
60 g/2-3 oz butter
salt and freshly ground pepper
2 tablespoons fine mustard
2 tablespoons coarse mustard
1½ tablespoons finely chopped
thyme
400 ml/14 fl oz white wine
150 ml/5 fl oz cream

Preparation/serving: approx.
1½ hours/10 minutes
Contains per serving: 2954 kJ/711 kcal.
51 g protein, 48 g fat, 2 g carbohydrate

Variations
* *Cook 150 g/5 oz stoned prunes*
along with the rabbit for
30 minutes, use red wine instead
of white and omit the mustard.
Garnish with crispy bacon rashers.
* *Instead of the mustard, add*
200 g/7 oz mushrooms and
2 tablespoons cognac 5 minutes
before the end of the cooking time.

Preparation. Blot the rabbit quarters dry with paper towel. Heat the butter in a large casserole and brown the rabbit on all sides over high heat. Remove from the dish, sprinkle with salt and pepper and brush the rabbit with the fine mustard.

• Stir the coarse mustard, thyme and white wine into the cooking fat and bring to the boil. Return the rabbit to the dish, cover, and cook gently over a low heat for about 1 hour until tender. Turn the rabbit frequently.

To serve. Remove the rabbit from the pan and keep warm under aluminium foil.

• Pour the cream into the cooking juices and slightly reduce the sauce over a high heat. Adjust seasoning.

• Put the rabbit on a warmed platter and cover with sauce.

• Delicious with braised savoy cabbage and rice.

Jugged hare

1 onion
1 chilli pepper
3-4 cloves
2 tablespoons finely chopped thyme
salt and freshly ground pepper
1 tablespoon red wine vinegar
500 ml/1 pint red wine
1 hare, cut in pieces
2 thick slices spicy cake
75 g/3 oz butter
100 g smoked bacon, cut into small pieces
3 tablespoons flour
1 small tin tomato puree

Preparation/cooking: approx. 20 mins/2 hours

Marinade: 8 hours

Contains per serving: 3210 kJ/768 kcal. 72 g protein, 34 g fat, 21 g carbohydrate

Variation
Remove the meat from the bones, cut into small pieces and return to the sauce. Add a dash of cream and serve in hot puff pastry cases.

Preparation. Peel and slice the onion. De-seed and finely slice the pepper. In a large bowl mix the onion and pepper with the cloves, thyme and 1 teaspoon salt and pepper. Add the vinegar and wine and put the hare pieces in the marinade. Cover with cling film and leave to marinate in the refrigerator for at least 8 hours (preferably longer).
• Cut the breakfast cake into small cubes.
• Remove the hare pieces from the marinade and blot dry with paper towel. Strain the marinade.
• Heat the butter in a large casserole and brown a few hare pieces at a time over a high heat. Remove from the pan.
• Fry the bacon pieces for 3 minutes in the remaining fat, stir in the flour and tomato puree and leave the roux to cook gently over a low heat for a few minutes.
• Slowly pour the strained marinade into this, stirring all the while with a whisk. Bring to the boil, still stirring, until a thick smooth sauce.
Cooking. Mix the cubed breakfast cake and hare through the sauce and leave covered over a low heat for 2 hours until hare is tender.
• Serve the meat on a large warmed platter and pass round the sauce separately.
• Delicious with stir-fried sprouts and potato puffs.

MEAT AND GAME DISHES

Spicy stew

500 g/1 lb onions
50 g/2 oz butter
750 g/1^1/$_2$ lb stewing beef
salt and freshly ground pepper
1 tablespoon flour
500 ml/1 pint beef stock
2 bay leaves
2-3 cloves
2 tablespoons vinegar
1 tub crème fraîche

Preparation/serving: approx.
3 hours/5 minutes
Contains per serving: 2164 kJ/520 kcal.
41 g protein, 37 g fat, 6 g carbohydrate

Preparation. Peel and slice the onion into rings.
• Heat the butter in a frying pan and brown the meat all over. Season with salt and pepper. Add the onion to the meat and continue frying a few minutes more. Sprinkle over the flour and mix everything together until brown.
• Heat the stock, add the bay leaves, cloves and vinegar and pour over the meat. Cover and simmer gently for about 2^1/$_2$-3 hours until cooked.
To serve. Remove the bay leaf and cloves from the stew and stir in the crème fraîche.
• Serve with boiled potatoes and red cabbage.

Variations
* Substitute red wine for half the stock. Use cocktail onions instead of
ordinary onions and add 300 g/10 oz baby carrots.
* Add ^{1}/$_2$ teaspoon ground coriander, 1 teaspoon cinnamon and
3 springs thyme to the stew.

Braised chicken with tutti-frutti

1 onion
100 g/3¹/₂ oz bacon
4 chicken legs
salt and freshly ground pepper
3 tablespoons flour
30 g/1 oz butter
¹/₄ l/¹/₂ pint vegetable stock
1 bay leaf
1 tablespoon fresh or 1 teaspoon dried thyme
250 g/8 oz mushrooms
For the tutti-frutti
250 g/8 oz tutti-frutti (dried
fruit), soaked in water for
8 hours with a cinnamon stick
1 grated rind of a lemon
8 g/3 teaspoons sugar
¹/₂ teaspoon vanilla essence

Preparation/cooking: approx.
1¹/₂ hours

Soaking time: approx. 8 hours

Contains per serving: 2329 kJ/556 kcal.
41 g protein, 26 g fat, 39 g carbo-
hydrate.

Preparation. Peel and finely slice the onion. Cut the bacon into small pieces. Season the chicken with salt and pepper and roll through the flour.
• Heat the butter in a large casserole and fry the chicken over a high heat until brown. Remove the legs and set apart. Sauté the onion and bacon in the chicken fat for about 3 minutes.
• Add the stock, bay leaf and thyme. Return the chicken to the pan. Cover and braise the chicken over a low heat for 40-45 minutes until tender, turning from time to time.
• Clean and slice the mushrooms and add to the chicken 10 minutes before the end of the cooking time.
To serve. Remove the cinnamon stick from the tutti-frutti and put the fruit (in its water), sugar and vanilla essence into a small pan. Bring to the boil and simmer gently for 20 minutes.
• Serve the chicken on plates and pass the tutti-frutti around separately. Delicious with white rice.

4 SERVINGS

Sautéed herbed potatoes with garlic cream

1 kg/2 lb potatoes
2 shallots
40 g/1¹/2 oz butter
1 tablespoon finely chopped thyme
1 tablespoon finely chopped parsley
1 tablespoon finely chopped chives
For the cream:
3 cloves garlic
150 ml/5 fl oz crème fraîche
50 ml/2 fl oz yoghurt
salt and freshly ground pepper
pinch paprika powder

Preparation/cooking: approx. 25 minutes

Contains per serving: 1522 kJ/364 kcal. 6 g protein, 22 g fat, 36 g carbohydrate

Preparation. Scrub the potatoes, leave unpeeled and cut into pieces all the same size. Cook for 7 minutes in barely enough water to cover. Drain thoroughly.

• Peel and finely chop the shallots. Heat the butter in a large pan until brown. Sauté the potatoes, shallots and thyme over a high heat for about 8 minutes until golden brown and cooked.

• Peel the cloves of garlic and press out into a small bowl. Stir in the crème fraîche and yoghurt and season to taste with salt, pepper and paprika powder.

To serve. Add the chopped parsley and chives to the sautéed potatoes and adjust seasoning. Serve with the garlic cream.

• Delicious with braised cod.

Variations
* Add 100 g/3¹/2 oz diced salami to the potatoes and stir 6 finely chopped sundried tomatoes and 1 tablespoon green pesto into the garlic cream.
* Fry 100 g/3¹/2 oz bacon rashers and 1 teaspoon curry powder with the potatoes and stir 2 spring onions, cut into rings, into the garlic cream.

Red cabbage salad

1 onion
400 g/14 oz red cabbage,
finely sliced
5 tablespoons sunflower oil
2 tablespoons lemon juice
2 tablespoons mayonnaise
1 teaspoon mustard
1 teaspoon cumin
25 g/1 oz peeled walnuts

*Preparation/serving: approx.
10 minutes*
Waiting time: about 2 hours
*Contains per serving: 1050 kJ/254 kcal.
3 g protein, 24 g fat,
6 g carbohydrate*

Preparation. Peel and finely chop the onion. Combine the cabbage and onion in a large dish. In a bowl mix together the oil, lemon juice, mayonnaise, mustard and cumin and stir the dressing into the cabbage. Leave for a minimum 2 hours for the dressing to be thoroughly absorbed. Garnish the salad with chopped walnuts.

Traditional potato puree

1 kg/2 lb potatoes
salt
200 ml/7 fl oz milk
50-75 g/2-3 oz butter
freshly ground pepper
nutmeg

*Preparation/serving: approx.
35/5 minutes*

*Contains per serving: 1238 kJ/295 kcal.
6 g protein, 14 g fat, 36 g carbohydrate*

Preparation. Peel the potatoes and cut into pieces. Cook with a pinch salt for about 25 minutes in just enough water to barely cover the potatoes.
• Heat the milk and butter in a saucepan. Drain the potatoes and leave to steam dry.
To serve. Finely mash the potatoes with a masher or press through a vegetable mill. Add the warm butter and milk and stir until smooth.
• Season to taste with salt, pepper and nutmeg.

Variations

* For extra flavour add 1^1/$_2$ teaspoon fine mustard to the puree.
* Stir a tablespoon chopped chives or parsley into the puree.
* Substitute cream or sour cream for milk.

Braised red cabbage with cinnamon and raisins

1 onion
2 apples
50 g/2 oz butter
800 g/1½ pound red cabbage, finely sliced
150 ml/5 fl oz orange juice
2 tablespoons soft brown sugar
1 tablespoon cinnamon
2 cloves
2 bay leaves
100 g/3½ oz raisins

Preparation/serving: approx. 40/5 minutes

Contains per serving: 1008 kJ/240 kcal. 4 g protein, 10 g fat, 34 g carbohydrate

Variation
Add 1 tablespoon finely chopped ginger just before serving.

Preparation. Peel and finely chop the onion. Peel, core and finely chop the apples. Melt half the butter in a large casserole and fry the onions and apples for about 4 minutes until soft. Add the cabbage, orange juice, sugar, cinnamon, cloves, bay leaves and raisins. Cover and braise over a low heat for 30 minutes until cooked, occasionally stirring the cabbage.

To serve. Remove the cloves and bay leaves and stir in the remaining butter. Serve the cabbage in a warmed dish.

• Delicious with stew.

Appeltjes onder de deken: Apples under the blankets

4 small Cox's Orange apples
50 g/2 oz raisins
80 g/3 oz sugar
1 teaspoon cinnamon
25 g/1 oz butter
40 g/1^1/$_2$ oz custard powder
800 ml/1^1/$_2$ pints milk

Preparation/cooking: approx. 15/30 minutes

Contains per serving: 1480 kJ/ 352 kcal. 8 g protein, 12 g fat, 54 g carbohydrate

Variation
Add finely chopped balls of stem ginger, Amaretti biscuits, or pecan nuts to the raisin stuffing. Place the apples in individual oven dishes. When baked pour fresh chilled custard sauce over apples.

Preparation. Preheat the oven to 175 ºC/375 ºF. Peel and core the fruit with an apple corer. In a bowl combine the raisins with the cinnamon and 2 tablespoons of sugar. Stuff the mixture into the centres of the apples.

• Lay the apples side by side in a greased shallow oven dish. Dot each apple with butter and bake for 30 minutes until done.

• In a small bowl blend the custard powder and remaining sugar with 100 ml/2^1/$_2$ fl oz milk until a smooth paste. Bring the rest of the milk to the boil in a pan and add the custard paste, stirring all the while. Continue stirring until the custard is thick and smooth.

To serve. Spoon the custard sauce over the apples and serve hot.

Stewed pears

1 kg/2 lb small stewing pears
3 cloves
1 piece of lemon rind
2 cinnamon sticks
50 g/2 oz soft brown sugar
200 ml/ 7 fl oz red wine
100 ml/3 ½ fl oz blackcurrant
liqueur
1 tablespoon potato flour or
arrowroot flour

*Preparation/cooking: approx. 2 3/4
hours*

*Contains per serving: 1101 kJ/ 261 kcal.
1 g protein, 0 g fat, 45 g carbohydrate*

Tip
*Also delicious with game
and stews.*

Preparation. Peel the pears with a paring knife and leave whole. Stab the lemon rind with the cloves. Put the pears, lemon zest, cinnamon sticks and sugar in a large pan and pour in the red wine and liqueur. Add enough water to just cover the pears. Bring to the boil and leave the pears to simmer, covered, for 2½ hours until tender.

To serve. Remove the zest and cinnamon sticks. Lift the pears carefully out of the pan and serve on an attractive platter.

• In a cup combine the potato flour with a little pear juice and return to the pan. Leave the juice to thicken to a nice smooth wine sauce, stirring all the while with a whisk. Pour this over the stewed pears and serve hot or cold.

• Serve with cinnamon ice cream and thick whipped cream. Garnish each pear with a sprig of mint.

HEARTY DESSERTS

Rijstebrij: Rice pudding with brown sugar

1 vanilla pod
1 litre/2 pints milk
150 g/5 oz pudding rice
4 tablespoons brown soft sugar
40 g/1½ butter
cinnamon powder

Preparation/cooking: approx. 1 hour
Contains per serving: 1690 kJ/403 kcal.
11 g protein, 17 g fat, 51 g carbo-
hydrate

Preparation. Split the vanilla pod open length-wise. Bring the milk with the vanilla pod in a heavy-bottomed saucepan to the boil. Stir in the rice and return to the boil while still stirring. Cook the rice over a low heat for about 50 minutes, stirring frequently.
• Remove the vanilla pod from the rice, scrape out the black seeds and stir into the pudding.
To serve. Spoon the hot rice into four sweet-dishes and sprinkle with brown sugar. Add a small knob of butter and dust with cinnamon powder.

Variations
Decorate the rice pudding with roasted, flaked almonds.
Alm's House rice: add a few saffron threads to the milk, which turns the pudding a lovely golden colour and gives it a special spicy taste. Delicious with fresh strawberries or apricot compote.

Semolina pudding with redcurrant sauce

1 lemon
800 m/1^1/$_2$ pints milk
80 g/3 oz semolina
125 g/4 oz sugar
^{1}/$_4$ litre/^{1}/$_2$ pint redcurrant or
blackcurrant dessert sauce
1 cinnamon stick
1 tablespoon potato flour or
arrowroot flour

Preparation/cooking: approx.
30 minutes
To set: 1-2 hours
Contains per serving: 1458 kJ/345 kcal.
9 g protein, 7 g fat, 61 g carbohydrate

Variation
Semolina pudding with almonds.
Finely ground 50 g/2 oz almonds in
a food processor and stir into the
hot semolina together with a
beaten egg yolk. Beat the egg
white until stiff and fold gently
into the nearly cold mixture. Turn
into a pudding mould.

Preparation. Wash the lemon and peel thinly. Bring the milk with half the lemon zest to the boil in a heavy-bottomed saucepan and leave to simmer gently for 10 minutes.

• Mix together the semolina and half the sugar in a small bowl. Remove the lemon zest from the milk and, while stirring, add the semolina mixture. Continue stirring until the semolina thickens and leave to cook gently over a low heat for another 8 minutes.

• Rinse a 1-litre/2 pint pudding mould in cold water. Pour the semolina mixture into the mould. Allow to cool and then refrigerate for 1-2 hours until set.

• In a saucepan bring the redcurrant sauce with 100 m /3^1/$_2$ fl oz water, cinnamon stick and remaining lemon zest to the boil. Then leave to simmer gently for 10 minutes, stirring from time to time.

• Remove cinnamon stick and lemon zest and dissolve the remaining sugar into the sauce. In a cup blend the potato flour with 1 tablespoon of water until smooth and add to the hot sauce, stirring all the while. Continue stirring until sauce is thoroughly blended. Allow to cool.

To serve. Turn the semolina pudding onto a dish and drizzle a little redcurrant sauce over it. Serve the remainder separately.

Schoenlapperstaart: Cobbler's cake

1 kg/2 1b of tart apples
1 packet of crispbakes
3 eggs
50 g/2 oz butter
100 g/$3^{1}/_{2}$ oz sugar
2 teaspoons cinnamon
1 teaspoon ginger powder
pinch of all spice
125 g/4 oz raisins
icing sugar

Preparation/cooking: approx.
$1^{1}/_{2}$ hours

Contains per serving: 1491 kJ/354 kcal.
8 g protein, 11 g fat, 57 g carbohydrate

Variation

Substitute 125 g/4 oz finely chop-
ped dried apricots for the raisins
and stir 6 finely chopped balls of
stem ginger into the apple mixture.

Preparation. Preheat the oven to 175 °C/375 °F.
Peel, core and slice the apples. Cook in a saucepan
with a little water until a thick purée. Crumble the
crispbakes. Separate the egg whites from the yolks
and beat in a clean bowl until stiff peaks are
formed. Lightly grease a 24 cm/8 in cake tin.
• Stir the crumbled crispbakes, butter, sugar, cinnamon, ginger powder, all spice, raisins and egg
yolks (beaten) into the apple purée. Gently fold in
the egg whites and pour the mixture into the cake
tin. Smooth over the surface with the flat surface
of a knife.
• Bake the tart in the middle of the oven for
50-60 minutes until golden brown and cooked.
To serve. Allow to cool and dust the tart liberally
with icing sugar.
• Delicious with fresh chilled custard sauce, lightly
whipped cream or ice cream.

Buttermilk pudding

2 lemons
12 sheets gelatine
125 g/4 oz sugar
1/2 litre/1 pint buttermilk
1/8 litre/1/4 pint whipping cream
2 packets vanilla sugar or
1 level tablespoon of sugar and
1 teaspoon vanilla essence
250 g/8 oz strawberries

*Preparation/cooking: approx.
25 minutes
To set : 3-4 hours*

*Contains per serving: 1330 kJ/316 kcal.
11 g protein, 12 g fat, 43 g carbohydrate*

Variation
*Yogurt pudding. Substitute yogurt
for the buttermilk and use 10
sheets of gelatine.
*Decorate with fresh raspberries
and sprigs of mint.*

Preparation. Cut a piece of zest, about 5 cm/2 in, from a lemon. Squeeze the juice of the lemons into a bowl. Bring 100 ml/3 1/2 fl oz of water to the boil with the zest and leave to simmer gently for 10 minutes to absorb the lemon flavour.

• Meanwhile soak the sheets of gelatine in a bowl of cold water for 5 minutes until soft. Remove the lemon zest from the water. Remove the pan from the heat. Drain the gelatine and stir into the hot liquid. Add the sugar and stir in the lemon juice. Pour in the buttermilk, while stirring all the time, and allow to cool until partly set.

• Lightly grease a 1 litre/2 pint, non-aluminium pudding mould and pour in the buttermilk mixture. Refrigerate for 3-4 hours until the pudding has set.

To serve. Whip the cream and vanilla sugar together until stiff. Wash the strawberries and remove tops. Carefully run a knife around the edge of the pudding. Place a flat serving-dish or large plate on top of the mould and reverse both so that the pudding slides out onto the dish.

• Decorate with strawberries and serve the vanilla whipped cream separately.

Hangop: Curd with prunes

2 litre/3 1/2 pints yogurt
1 orange
1/4 litre/1/2 pint red wine or tea
250 g/8 oz dried stoned prunes,
soaked
2 packets vanilla sugar or
1 level tablespoon of sugar and
1 teaspoon vanilla essence
1/2 teaspoon mixed spice

*Preparation/cooking: approx. 30 minutes
Contains per serving: 1936 kJ/461 kcal.
19 g protein, 15 g fat, 52 g carbohydrate*

Variations

* As a summer treat serve the curd
with a fresh red fruit salad of
strawberries, raspberries, red-
currants and blueberries.
* Curd can be served traditionally
with a (Dutch) crispbake and
brown soft sugar.

Preparation. Wet a piece of muslin or clean tea towel and squeeze out thoroughly. Line a colander with the cloth and pour in the yogurt. Allow the yogurt to drain for a few hours until thick and creamy.
• Wash the orange and grate the rind. Press the juice out of the orange.
• In a saucepan bring the orange juice, wine, grated zest, prunes, vanilla sugar and mixed spice to the boil. Leave the mixture to simmer over a low heat for 15-20 minutes, until the liquid has almost evaporated and the prunes are covered in a syrupy sauce. Leave to cool.

To serve. Divide the curd into 4 sweet-dishes and spoon the prunes and sauce over it.

4 SERVINGS

500 g/1 lb rhubarb
75 ml/3 fl oz red grape juice
sugar
1 tablespoon custard powder
2 egg whites
120 g/4 oz icing sugar
1/2 teaspoon cornflour
1/2 teaspoon vinegar

*Preparation/cooking: approx.
15/20 minutes*

*Contains per serving: 820 kJ/193 kcal.
3 g protein, 0 g fat, 45 g carbohydrate*

Variation

*Add 250 g/8 oz of washed straw-
berries and a dash of strawberry
liqueur to the rhubarb compote.*

Preparation. Preheat the oven to 175 °C/375 °F.
Wash the rhubarb stalks and cut into small chunks.
• In a large saucepan bring the rhubarb and grape
juice to the boil. Cook for a further 5-6 minutes
until tender. The liquid should have evaporated.
• Remove the pan from the heat and stir in the
custard powder and add sugar to taste. Transfer
the rhubarb to a shallow baking dish.
• In a clean bowl (remove any trace of grease with
lemon juice), beat the egg whites until stiff. Add
some of the icing sugar, cornflour and vinegar and
beat until a firm sticky mass, gradually adding the
remaining sugar. Continue beating until the mixture has a nice gloss to it.
Cooking. Spread the peaks of egg white over the
rhubarb and bake in an oven for 20-30 minutes until
the egg white is set and crisp. Serve immediately.
• Delicious with fresh chilled custard sauce.

HEARTY DESSERTS

Nutrition information

The recipes in this book are accompanied by a nutrition calculation giving the energy, protein, carbohydrate and fat content per serving. In order to help you link the nutritional content of the recipes with average recommended daily allowance, information on the most important nutrients and vitamins are given below. See page 66 for further information on energy and energy requirements.

Proteins

We use proteins for building and maintaining the body. They are essential for virtually all living organisms. While proteins are extremely important, it doesn't imply you need to eat a lot of them, since the body converts an excess of these (see chart) into fatty tissue. Proteins are found in meat, fish, poultry, dairy products, beans and nuts. There are also various protein products like tofu, tempeh and quorn.

Carbohydrates

Carbohydrates such as starch and sugars are major energy providers. Sugars burn up more quickly than starches, so that the latter are the most important for sustained energy production. Starch is found namely in potatoes, grain products (rice, pasta and bread etc) and beans, whereas sugars are found in such foodstuffs as fruit, milk and granulated sugar. Dietary fibre is an indigestible carbohydrate found in vegetables, fruits and whole grain products. It aids digestion and creates a satisfied feeling in the stomach.

Fats

Fats also provide energy and contain substances the body needs. Fats preserve heat and are important for carrying and storing fat-soluble vitamins. There are fats with saturated fatty acids and those with non-saturated fatty acids. Saturated fats are mostly from animal sources, but also, for instance, from coconut. The general view that saturated fats increase the risk of heart and vascular decease is not true of all saturated fats. Unsaturated fats are usually from vegetable sources and oily fish. These fatty acids reduce the risk of heart and vascular decease.

Daily average allowance

	Protein gram	Fat gram	Carbohydrate gram
Women			
19-22 jr	60	80	310
22-50 jr	55	75	290
50-65 jr	52	70	280
65+	52	65	260
Men			
19-22 jr	79	105	400
22-50 jr	71	95	370
50-65 jr	64	90	330
65+	56	75	290

Recommended daily intake of fluid: $1^1/_2$ litres (3 pints), excluding alcohol, tea and coffee which cause dehydration.